ALTA CALIFORNIA

Missions of the
Southern
Coast

San Francisco Solano

San Rafael Arcangel

San Francisco de Asis

San Jose de Guadalupe

Santa Clara de Asis

Santa Cruz

San Juan Bautista

San Carlos Borromeo de Carmelo

Nuestra Senora de la Soledad

San Antonio de Padua

San Miguel Arcangel

San Luis Obispo de Tolosa

La Purisima Concepcion de Maria Santisima

Santa Ines Virgen y Martir

Santa Barbara Virgen y Martir

San Buenaventura

San Fernando Rey de Espana

San Gabriel Arcangel

San Juan Capistrano

San Luis Rey de Francia

San Diego de Alcala

California
MISSIONS

Missions of the
Southern
Coast

Nancy Lemke

LERNER PUBLICATIONS COMPANY

Series editors: Elizabeth Verdick, Karen Chernyaev, Mary M. Rodgers
Series photo researcher: Amy Cox
Series designer: Zachary Marell

Every effort has been made to secure permission for the quoted material and for the photographs in this book.

Cover: At San Diego de Alcalá, the first mission founded in what is now the state of California, a white-washed wall contrasts sharply with the carved oak door of the church. Title page: Bell ringers at San Juan Capistrano sounded the mission's bells by pulling on ropes attached to the clappers (bells' tongues).

LIBRARY OF CONGRESS CATALOGING-IN-PUBLICATION DATA

Lemke, Nancy, 1949–
    Missions of the southern coast / by Nancy Lemke.
        p.   cm.—(California missions)
    Includes index.
    Summary: Charts the histories of the California missions of San Diego de Alcalá, San Juan Capistrano, and San Luis Rey de Francia and briefly describes life among the Native Americans of southwestern California before the arrival of the Spaniards.
    ISBN 0–8225–1925–9 (lib. bdg.)
    1. Spanish mission buildings—California—Pacific Coast—Juvenile literature.
2. California—History—To 1846—Juvenile literature. [1. Missions—California.
2. California—History. 3. Indians of North America—Missions—California.]
    I. Title. II. Series.
F862.L49 1996
979.4'902—dc20   95–16619
                                                                      CIP
                                                                      AC

Manufactured in the United States of America
1 2 3 4 5 6 – JR – 01 00 99 98 97 96

CONTENTS

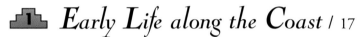

GLOSSARY

adobe: A type of clay soil found in Mexico and in dry parts of the United States. In Alta California, workers formed wet adobe into bricks that hardened in the sun.

Alta California (Upper California): An old Spanish name for the present-day state of California.

Baja California (Lower California): A strip of land off the northwestern coast of Mexico that lies between the Pacific Ocean and the Gulf of California. Part of Mexico, Baja California borders the U.S. state of California.

Franciscan: A member of the Order of Friars Minor, a Roman Catholic community founded in Italy by Saint Francis of Assisi in 1209. The Franciscans are dedicated to performing missionary work and acts of charity.

mission: A center where missionaries (religious teachers) work to spread their beliefs to other people and to teach a new way of life.

missionary: A person sent out by a religious group to spread its beliefs to other people.

neophyte: A Greek word meaning "newly converted" that refers to an Indian baptized into the Roman Catholic community.

New Spain: A large area once belonging to Spain that included what are now the southwestern United States and Mexico. After 1821, when New Spain had gained its independence from the Spanish Empire, the region became known as the Republic of Mexico.

presidio: A Spanish fort for housing soldiers. In Alta California, Spaniards built presidios to protect the missions and priests from possible attacks and to enforce order in the region. California's four main presidios were located at San Diego, Santa Barbara, Monterey, and San Francisco.

quadrangle: A four-sided enclosure surrounded by buildings.

reservation: Tracts of land set aside by the U.S. government to be used by Native Americans.

secularization: A series of laws enacted by the Mexican government in the 1830s. The rulings aimed to take mission land and buildings from Franciscan control and to place the churches in the hands of parish priests, who didn't perform missionary work. Much of the land was distributed to families and individuals.

PRONUNCIATION GUIDE*

Cabrillo, Juan Rodríguez	kah-BREE-yoh, WAHN roh-DREE-gays
Diegueños	dee-ay-GAY-nyos
El Camino Reál	el kah-MEE-no ray-AHL
Jayme, Luís	HY-may, loo-EES
Juaneños	wah-NAY-nyos
Lasuén, Fermín de	lah-soo-AYN, fair-MEEN day
Luiseños	loo-ee-SAY-nyos
Peyri, Antonio	PAY-ree, ahn-TOH-nee-oh
Portolá, Gaspar de	por-toh-LAH, gahs-PAHR day
San Diego de Alcalá	SAHN dee-AY-go day ahl-kah-LAH
San Juan Capistrano	SAHN WAHN kah-pees-TRAH-noh
San Luis Rey de Francia	SAHN loo-EES RAY day FRAHN-see-ah
Serra, Junípero	SEH-rrah, hoo-NEE-pay-roh
Vizcaíno, Sebastián	vees-kah-EE-no, say-bahs-tee-AHN

* Local pronunciations may differ.

PREFACE

The religious beliefs and traditions of the Indians of California teach that the blessings of a rich land and a mild climate are gifts from the Creator. The Indians show their love and respect for the Creator—and for all of creation—by carefully managing the land for future generations and by living in harmony with the natural environment.

Over the course of many centuries, the Indians of California organized small, independent societies. Only in the hot, dry deserts of southeastern California did they farm the land to feed themselves. Elsewhere, the abundance of fish, deer, antelope, waterfowl, and wild seeds supplied all that the Indians needed for survival. The economies of these societies did not create huge surpluses of food. Instead the people produced only what they expected would meet their needs. Yet there is no record of famine during the long period when Indians in California managed the land.

These age-old beliefs and practices stood in sharp contrast to the policies of the Spaniards who began to settle areas of California in the late 1700s. Spain established religious missions along the coast to anchor its empire in California. At these missions, Spanish priests baptized thousands of Indians into the Roman Catholic religion. Instead of continuing to hunt and gather their food, the Indians were made to work on mission estates where farming supported the settlements. Pastures for mission livestock soon took over Indian land, and European farming activities depleted native plants. Illnesses that the Spaniards had unintentionally carried from Europe brought additional suffering to many Indian groups.

The Indians living in California numbered 340,000 in the late 1700s, but only 100,000 remained after roughly 70 years of Spanish missionization. Many of the Indians died from disease. Spanish soldiers killed other Indians during native revolts at the missions. Some entire Indian societies were wiped out.

Thousands of mission Indian descendants proudly continue to practice their native culture and to speak their native language. But what is most important to these survivors is that their people's history be understood by those who now call California home, as well as by others across the nation. Through this series of books, young readers will learn for the first time how the missions affected the Indians and their traditional societies.

Perhaps one of the key lessons to be learned from an honest and evenhanded account of California's missions is that the Indians had something important to teach the Spaniards and the people who came to the region later. Our ancestors and today's elders instill in us that we must respect and live in harmony with animals, plants, and one another. While this is an ancient wisdom, it seems especially relevant to our future survival.

Professor Edward D. Castillo
Cahuilla-Luiseño Mission Indian Descendant

INTRODUCTION

FOUNDED BY SPAIN, THE CALIFORNIA **MISSIONS** ARE located on a narrow strip of California's Pacific coast. Some of the historic buildings sit near present-day Highway 101, which roughly follows what was once a roadway called El Camino Reál (the Royal Road), so named to honor the king of Spain. The trail linked a chain of 21 missions set up between 1769 and 1823.

Spain, along with leaders of the Roman Catholic Church, established missions and *presidios* (forts) throughout the Spanish Empire to strengthen its claim to the land. In the 1600s, Spain built mission settlements on the peninsula known as **Baja California,** as well as in other areas of **New Spain** (present-day Mexico).

The goal of the Spanish mission system in North America was to make Indians accept Spanish ways and become loyal subjects of the Spanish king. Priests functioning as **missionaries** (religious teachers) tried to convert the local Indian populations to Catholicism and to

In the mid-1700s, Native Americans living in what is now California came into contact with Roman Catholic missionaries from Spain.

11

In this nineteenth-century drawing, soldiers aim their guns at an Indian who is trying to escape from a mission. Some Native Americans joined the missions by choice, but many others were forced to live and work at the religious settlements.

teach them to dress and behave like Spaniards. Soldiers came to protect the missionaries and to make sure the Indians obeyed the priests.

During the late 1700s, Spain wanted to spread its authority northward from Baja California into the region known as **Alta California,** where Spain's settlement pattern would be repeated. The first group of Spanish soldiers and missionaries traveled to Alta California in 1769. The missionaries, priests of the **Franciscan** order, were led by Junípero Serra, the father-president of the mission system.

The soldiers and missionaries came into contact with communities of Native Americans, or Indians, that dotted the coastal and inland areas of Alta California. For thousands of years, the region had been home to many Native American groups that spoke a wide variety of languages. Using these Indians as unpaid laborers was vital to the success of the mission system. The mission economy was based on agriculture—a way of life unfamiliar to local Indians, who mostly hunted game and gathered wild plants for food.

Although some Indians willingly joined the missions, the Franciscans relied on various methods to convince or force other Native Americans to become part of the mission system. The priests sometimes lured Indians with gifts of glass beads and colored cloth or other items new to the Native Americans. Some Indians who lost their hunting and food-gathering grounds to mission farms and ranches joined the Spanish settlements to survive. In other cases, Spanish soldiers forcibly took villagers from their homes.

Neophytes, or Indians recruited into the missions, were expected to learn the Catholic faith and the skills for farming and building. Afterward—Spain reasoned—the Native Americans would be able to manage the property themselves, a process that officials figured would take 10 years. But a much different turn of events took place.

Highlights of Present-Day California

- • City
- Mission (see list below left)
- County
- El Camino Reál
- U.S. highway

Miles
0 20 40 60 80 100

0 40 80 120
Kilometers

CALIFORNIA MISSIONS

- A San Francisco Solano
- B San Rafael Arcángel
- C San Francisco de Asís
- D San José de Guadalupe
- E Santa Clara de Asís
- F Santa Cruz
- G San Juan Bautista
- H San Carlos Borromeo
- I Soledad
- J San Antonio de Padua
- K San Miguel Arcángel
- L San Luis Obispo
- M La Purísima
- N Santa Inés
- O Santa Bárbara
- P San Buenaventura
- Q San Fernando Rey
- R San Gabriel Arcángel
- S San Juan Capistrano
- T San Luis Rey de Francia
- U San Diego de Alcalá

NEVADA

★ Sacramento

Bodega Bay

Sonoma

San Pablo Bay

San Rafael
SAN FRANCISCO PRESIDIO

Alcatraz I.

San Francisco

Fremont

San Francisco Bay

Guadalupe R.

San Jose

Santa Clara

San Lorenzo

Santa Cruz

Pajaro R.

San Juan Bautista

Monterey Bay

MONTEREY PRESIDIO

Monterey

Carmel

Carmel R.

Salinas R.

Soledad

San

King City

San Antonio R.

Nacimiento R.

San Miguel

Sacramento River

Stanislaus R.

San Joaquin River

SIERRA NEVADA

CALIFORNIA

San Joaquin Valley

COAST RANGE

PACIFIC OCEAN

San Luis Obispo

La Purísima

Lompoc

Solvang

Santa Ynez

VENTURA COUNTY

Santa Barbara Presidio

Point Conception

Santa Ynez R.

Santa Barbara

SANTA BARBARA CHANNEL

Ventura R.

Ventura

San Buenaventura

Santa Clara R.

San Fernando

Los Angeles R.

San Gabriel R.

San Gabriel

MOJAVE DESERT

San Miguel I.

Santa Rosa I.

Santa Cruz I.

Anacapa Is.

Santa Monica Bay

SANTA BARBARA ISLANDS

Santa Barbara I.

San Nicolas I.

San Clemente I.

Los Angeles

Santa Catalina I.

ORANGE COUNTY

Santa Ana R.

San Juan Capistrano

Oceanside

San Luis Rey de Francia

San Diego

San Diego R.

San Diego Presidio

San Diego Bay

N

UNITED STATES

MEXICO

MEXICO

BAJA CALIFORNIA

PACIFIC OCEAN

CALIFORNIA MISSION	FOUNDING DATE
San Diego de Alcalá	July 16, 1769
San Carlos Borromeo de Carmelo	June 3, 1770
San Antonio de Padua	July 14, 1771
San Gabriel Arcángel	September 8, 1771
San Luis Obispo de Tolosa	September 1, 1772
San Francisco de Asís	June 29, 1776
San Juan Capistrano	November 1, 1776
Santa Clara de Asís	January 12, 1777
San Buenaventura	March 31, 1782
Santa Bárbara Virgen y Mártir	December 4, 1786
La Purísima Concepción de Maria Santísima	December 8, 1787
Santa Cruz	August 28, 1791
Nuestra Señora de la Soledad	October 9, 1791
San José de Guadalupe	June 11, 1797
San Juan Bautista	June 24, 1797
San Miguel Arcángel	July 25, 1797
San Fernando Rey de España	September 8, 1797
San Luis Rey de Francia	June 13, 1798
Santa Inés Virgen y Mártir	September 17, 1804
San Rafael Arcángel	December 14, 1817
San Francisco Solano	July 4, 1823

Forced to abandon their villages and to give up their age-old traditions, many Native Americans didn't adjust to mission life. In fact, most Indians died soon after entering the missions—mainly from European diseases that eventually killed thousands of Indians throughout California.

Because hundreds of Indian laborers worked at each mission, most of the settlements thrived. The missions produced grapes, olives, wheat, cattle hides, cloth, soap, candles, and other goods. In fact, the missions successfully introduced to Alta California a variety of crops and livestock that still benefit present-day Californians.

The missions became so productive that the Franciscans es-

(Facing page) **California's vineyards partly owe their beginnings to the Spanish missionaries, who raised grapes and other fruit crops.**

tablished a valuable trade network. Mission priests exchanged goods and provided nearby soldiers and settlers with provisions. The agricultural wealth of the missions angered many settlers and soldiers, who resented the priests for holding Alta California's most fertile land and the majority of the livestock and for controlling the Indian labor force.

This resentment grew stronger after 1821, when New Spain became the independent country of Mexico. Mexico claimed Alta California and began the **secularization** of the missions. The mission churches still offered religious services, but the Spanish Franciscans were to be replaced by secular priests. These priests weren't missionaries seeking to convert people.

By 1836 the neophytes were free to leave the missions, and the settlements quickly declined from the loss of workers. Few of the former neophytes found success away from the missions, however. Many continued as forced laborers on *ranchos* (ranches) or in nearby *pueblos* (towns), earning little or no pay.

In 1848 Mexico lost a war against the United States and ceded Alta California to the U.S. government. By that time, about half of Alta California's Indian population had died. Neophytes who had remained at the missions often had no village to which to return. They moved to pueblos or to inland areas. Meanwhile, the missions went into a state of decay, only to be rebuilt years later.

This book will focus on the three missions at the southern end of California's coast. Missionaries founded San Diego de Alcalá, the first and southernmost mission in the chain, in 1769. San Juan Capistrano is north of San Diego and was set up as the seventh mission in 1776. San Luis Rey de Francia, the eighteenth mission, was built in 1798 between San Diego de Alcalá and San Juan Capistrano.

PART ONE

Early Life along the Coast

BETWEEN THE PACIFIC OCEAN AND THE COASTAL mountain ranges of southwestern California, the landscape looks like a wrinkled bedsheet. Shallow canyons and valleys dip between steep, flat-topped hills called mesas. Creeks and rivers flow swiftly through the area during the rainy season (winter and early spring) and dry up from the warmth of the summer sun. The area has mild temperatures year-round.

On the oceanfront, sand and rocky soil cover wide beaches. The salty waters are home to shellfish such as abalones and lobsters. Whales swim offshore, and seals gather on the beach to bask in the sun.

Shoshonean- and Yuman-speakers—the Indians who lived in the southern coast region—fished along beaches strewn with huge, wave-sculpted boulders. The area's plants and animals included prickly pear cacti and howling coyotes.

17

Inland from the coast, the terrain gradually rises. Here the summers are hotter and the winters cooler. Little rain falls, except during the rainy season. Huge boulders dot the landscape. Deer and mountain lions roam across grassy meadows and take shelter under large, twisted oak trees.

In the rugged coastal ranges, pine trees join the oaks. Sure-footed mountain sheep leap up and down the mountainsides. Just east of the mountains, the land drops 6,000 feet into a hot, sandy desert. Coyotes, kangaroo rats, and tiny antelope squirrels prowl among the prickly cacti.

Much of the southwestern region of California is covered by chaparrals, or areas made up of scrubby bushes that thrive in the dry summer heat. The chaparral spreads over the ground like a head-high carpet. Although the bushes look lifeless, they are home to many kinds of birds. Snakes slither along the ground, and rabbits, skunks, rats, and lizards scurry among the dense plants.

The People

Native Americans were the first people to settle the warm southwestern region. During the 1500s, an estimated 7,000 Indians lived here. Their distant ancestors had probably arrived in the area thousands of years earlier from the north and the east.

These Native Americans spoke dialects that came from two main languages—Shoshonean and Yuman. Most of the Yuman-speakers settled near what is now San Diego, while Shoshonean-speakers made their homes directly north.

Although they spoke different languages, the groups shared a common lifestyle. For example, they formed small bands, or tribelets, that each had about 100 to 500 people. Tribelet members lived in villages. Many tribelets took the name of their

A mountain lion takes shelter from the heat beneath a rock overhang.

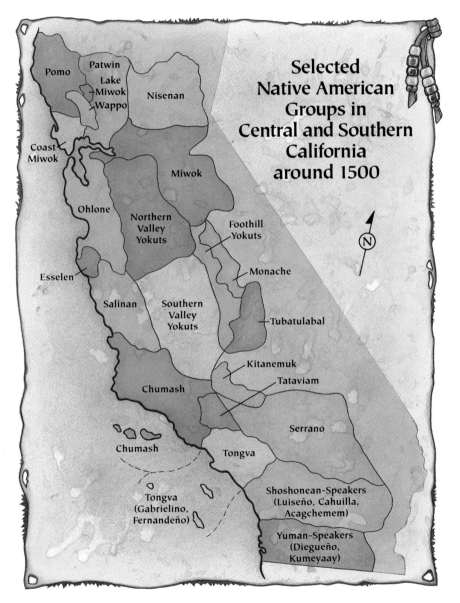

Selected Native American Groups in Central and Southern California around 1500

Pomo

Patwin
Lake
Miwok
Wappo

Nisenan

Coast
Miwok

Miwok

Ohlone

Northern
Valley
Yokuts

Foothill
Yokuts

Monache

Esselen

Salinan

Southern
Valley
Yokuts

Tubatulabal

Kitanemuk
Tataviam

Chumash

Serrano

Chumash

Tongva

Tongva
(Gabrielino,
Fernandeño)

Shoshonean-Speakers
(Luiseño, Cahuilla,
Acagchemem)

Yuman-Speakers
(Diegueño,
Kumeyaay)

Ⓝ

village or else simply called themselves "the people."

Indian Communities

The Shoshonean- and Yuman-speakers usually set up their villages along creeks or on river-banks, where a fresh water supply was available. They built dome-shaped houses, lashing sticks together to create a wooden frame. The Indians then tied reeds or other grasses over the frame. Sometimes the builders added a layer of soil on top of these materials to keep out rain and wind. When the homes got too dirty or full of bugs, the Indians burned the structures and made new ones.

The Indians' way of life fit the seasons and the environment. Because the weather in the region was usually mild, both Shoshonean- and Yuman-speakers wore few clothes.

Women dressed in skirts made from reeds, rabbit skins, or the

19

Tough agave plants *(above)* not only were a source of food for the Indians but also provided the raw materials for making sandals. Hunters used throwing sticks *(right)* to kill rabbits and other small game.

plants for food. Chaparral bushes, for example, provided seeds and berries. The main food source, though, was acorns from oak trees. Each fall families trekked into the mountains to collect the abundant nuts.

In the villages, acorns were stored in huge, round baskets.

After gathering acorns, the Indians stored the nuts in woven containers called granaries.

soft inner bark of willow trees. Men often wore only a belt in which they carried knives, food, and tools. Children aged 10 and younger went naked. In colder weather, capes and blankets made from animal skins kept the people warm.

When hunting in the desert, Indian men sometimes put on sandals to protect their feet from the hot sand. The Native Americans crafted these shoes from agave—a large desert plant with tough fibers. Rich in nutrients, agave was also cooked to make a sweet, pulpy treat.

Shoshonean- and Yuman-speakers caught fish and shellfish from the ocean. Hunters stalked birds, rabbits, deer, and other animals using nets, arrows, and slings. The tribelets also gathered roots, herbs, and other

Eating Acorns

In autumn Indians journeyed into the mountains to gather acorns from oak trees. The Native Americans hit the trees with sticks and collected the nuts that fell to the ground. The people then split the shells with a stone. Getting the acorns ready to eat was a big job. To grind the nut meat into a fine powder, Indian women beat the acorns on top of a boulder with a stone pestle (pounding tool). The women used the same boulders each year, creating bowl-shaped dips in the worn rocks. The resulting powder—also called meal—tasted bitter from the acid in the nuts. To get rid of the bitterness, Indians placed the meal in a basket or in a hole lined with leaves. They then continually rinsed the mixture with water. Afterward, a cook placed the acorn meal in a clay pot over a fire, heating the powder into a porridge. Acorn mush could be eaten plain or flavored with berries, seeds, or dried meat.

To protect the nuts from hungry animals, Indians placed the baskets in trees, hid them in caves, or set them on poles above the ground. Animal skins on top of the baskets kept out the rain. A small hole in the bottom of each container could be uncovered to let the nuts drop out.

During years with plenty of rain, the oak trees and the chaparral thrived and provided a good supply of food. But sometimes the rainy season brought little water, and it was harder to find nuts, seeds, and other things to eat. The lack of food weakened the people, and some grew sick and died. During these hard times, they relied on the knowledge of their shamans, or healers.

The shamans performed religious ceremonies, healed the sick, and located food sources. The people depended on the shamans to tell them when to burn the chaparral and where to find the best hunting spots. The shamans shared their age-old

During ceremonial dances, shamans (religious leaders) wore skirts adorned with feathers.

Burning the Chaparrals

The Native Americans regularly burned the chaparral bushes, but it's not known for sure why they did this. Some experts think that setting fire to the dense plants was a way to improve the food supply, because tender new shoots sprouted after the brush had been burned away.

Other scholars believe that Indian hunters used the smoke to scare rabbits out of underground burrows. Whatever the reason, the fires were sometimes large. In fact, the first Spaniards to reach present-day southern California wrote about seeing huge clouds of smoke.

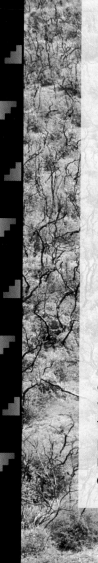

knowledge with just a few children, whom they carefully trained to carry on the teachings in the future.

Among the teachings were sacred songs and dances that went with religious ceremonies. For some rituals, the people decorated themselves with body paint. Many Indians painted their faces every day. Others marked their bodies with charcoal tattoos, poking dyes into their skin with a cactus needle or a sharp bone.

Indians of the southwestern region worshiped their Creators, who were thought to have made the land, people, animals, and plants. Believing that every living thing had a spirit, Native Americans expressed great respect for nature and all its power.

For example, if hunters killed a deer, they thanked the animal's spirit for providing food and skins. People who gathered nuts, berries, and other plant foods were careful to take only what they needed for survival. In this way, Indians of the southern coast region protected their environment and their natural resources.

Strangers Arrive

During the 1500s, rumors passed from village to village that strangers had been spotted along the coast. These newcomers were explorers from the Spanish colony, or settlement, of New Spain. The shiny steel armor that the travelers wore for protection reminded the Indians of the hard shell of a bug.

One explorer was Juan Rodríguez Cabrillo, the first European to land on the southern coast of Alta California. He arrived in 1542, seeking a water route through North America. Although Cabrillo met Indians on the coast, he didn't respect their rights to the land. He claimed the region for the Spanish king and sailed away.

Yuman-speakers used deer-hoof rattles in religious rituals and in celebrations.

In 1602 Sebastián Vizcaíno, another Spanish explorer, set foot on the Indians' homeland. He sailed into a large bay, gave the port the name San Diego, and continued northward.

Spain then lost interest in this faraway land. But in the mid-1700s, Russian hunters in search of fur-bearing animals began to explore the Pacific coast. When King Charles III of Spain heard word of their movements, he grew angry. To prevent foreigners from gaining a foothold on his territory, the king decided to establish Spanish settlements in Alta California.

A Catholic monarch, King Charles was closely connected with the Roman Catholic Church. Like the king, the pope (the church's leader) and other powerful religious officials wanted to spread their influence and beliefs to other parts of the world. The Spaniards decided to use the new settlements in Alta California as a way of gaining new converts (followers) to the Catholic faith.

The settlements needed people to build churches, to farm the land, and to set up towns. Although people from New Spain would help settle the new communities, Spanish officials also intended to make the Indi-ans in Alta California into Span-ish citizens. As part of this process, the Indians would have to follow the Roman Catholic religion—just as other Spanish citizens did.

To become Spanish citizens, the Indians also would have to learn to speak Spanish and to dress in European-style cloth-ing. More importantly, they would have to learn new skills such as farming. Because the financial success of the new settlements relied on a source of abundant labor, Spanish officials intended to make Indians in the coastal region become workers. Spanish leaders didn't care that the Native Americans already had their own way of life—one that had successfully supported Indian communities for thousands of years.

Shoshonean- and Yuman-speaking groups traditionally didn't give themselves tribal names. Instead they usually identified themselves by their village or their territory. But when the Spaniards arrived in the 1700s, they named the local Indians after the various missions. Along the southern coast, Native Americans came to be called Diegueños, Juaneños, and Luiseños.

Descendants of Yuman-speakers are now known by different names, including Kumeyaay. Many descendants of Shoshonean-speakers near Mission San Juan Capistrano use the title Acagchemem. Indians whose ancestors lived at Mission San Luis Rey have generally come to accept the name Luiseño.

First spotted and claimed by the explorer Juan Cabrillo in 1542, the wide, natural harbor of San Diego again attracted foreigners in the mid-1700s.

Junípero Serra, a member of the Franciscan religious order, was among the group of strangers who arrived in the southern coast region in 1769. His dream was to set up missions and to make the local Indians accept the Roman Catholic faith. The 56-year-old priest was considered too old, however, to face the rough living conditions in Alta California (modern California). At one point, he was so ill that the soldiers accompanying Serra urged him to give up. The priest's response was firm, "I shall not turn back. They can bury me wherever they wish." In fact, Serra went on to found nine missions. He died in 1784.

The First Mission

Dusting off the old maps drawn earlier by Cabrillo and Vizcaíno, Spanish officials studied Alta California. The maps showed two natural harbors where ships could easily drop off supplies. One port was located in San Diego. The other harbor, at Monterey Bay, lay far to the north of San Diego.

Two men from New Spain—Captain Gaspar de Portolá and Father Junípero Serra—were chosen to help secure Spain's claim to Alta California. Father Serra, a Catholic priest, belonged to the Franciscan religious order. As a missionary, or religious teacher, he had worked to spread his faith to Indians in New Spain.

Spanish officials sent Father Serra north to San Diego and Monterey to found missions. His job was to convert Indians near the missions to the Roman Catholic faith. Captain Portolá and a handful of other soldiers agreed to set up presidios near the missions. The presidios

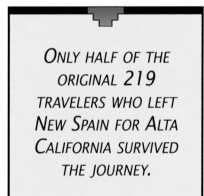

ONLY HALF OF THE ORIGINAL *219* TRAVELERS WHO LEFT NEW SPAIN FOR ALTA CALIFORNIA SURVIVED THE JOURNEY.

would protect the *padres* (meaning "fathers" in Spanish) and ensure that the Indians obeyed the Spaniards. According to the plan, the missions would eventually be turned into pueblos, towns that would be inhabited by Indians and Spanish settlers alike.

In 1769 the soldiers and missionaries began the long overland march up the coast—but they left without Father Serra. They had convinced the priest to stay behind because his leg was badly swollen with sores. Little did they know that Father Serra would make the treacherous journey anyway by mule. Other members of the expedition, as well as supplies, were sent on three ships.

The trip was long and difficult for all of these traveling groups. One ship was lost at sea. Many of the sailors on the other vessels died from scurvy, a sickness caused by a lack of the vitamin C found in fresh fruits and vegetables. And the weary overland group—including Father Serra—journeyed for many weeks across the hot desert before reaching San Diego.

A few miles from San Diego Bay, the travelers found a river lined with cottonwood trees. Along the banks, in a village

Some Yuman-speakers built their villages near the banks of the San Diego River to take advantage of the fresh supply of water.

Many of the Yuman-speaking Indians in Alta California came to believe that the Spaniards were powerful, but evil, shamans. The soldiers, for example, had tamed horses, something the Indians in the area had never done. And the newcomers' guns wounded or killed Native Americans.

Moreover, the Spaniards pointed at villagers. The Indians believed this foreign gesture sent sickness or harm. In the face of such power, the custom of the Yuman-speakers was to go to their shamans for healing.

Villagers constructed their dome-shaped homes of sticks and reeds. If the houses became too dirty or bug-ridden, they were burned and rebuilt.

called Cosoy, stood the dome-shaped houses of Yuman-speakers. Indian families carefully watched the newcomers scouting the area. Some of the Yuman-speakers found it unusual that no women traveled with the strangers and wondered if the visitors were a war party planning an attack.

Not far from the Indian village, the missionaries, sailors, and soldiers built temporary shelters overlooking the bay. Using brush and soil, they constructed huts, sickrooms, and a chapel. On July 16, 1769, Father Serra planted a cross next to the chapel and said the Catholic mass. This religious service formally established San Diego de Alcalá—the first California mission.

PART TWO

Missions of the Southern Coast

LOCATED ALONG THE SOUTHERNMOST POINTS OF El Camino Reál, the missions of San Diego de Alcalá, San Luis Rey de Francia, and San Juan Capistrano may be characterized as the "southern coast missions." Soldiers stationed at a presidio in San Diego protected these missions, around which pueblos eventually sprang up.

Because San Diego de Alcalá was the first mission in what is now California, the settlement had more difficulty getting started than did the missions that followed. For example, the region's poor soil

Flowers bloom in front of the church at San Diego de Alcalá, the first mission that Father Serra founded. The mission is named for Saint Didacus, a fifteenth-century monk whose work took him not only throughout his native Spain but also to Spain's island colonies in the Atlantic Ocean.

supported few crops, and nearby Native Americans repeatedly attacked the mission. San Juan Capistrano, on the other hand, prospered from the very beginning and became known for its beautiful architecture. Mission San Luis Rey de Francia also flourished—in large part because of the leadership of its head priest, Father Antonio Peyri. All three southern coast missions stand as monuments to a rich and complex piece of California's past.

Mission San Diego de Alcalá

Father Serra was pleased with the mission site for San Diego de Alcalá. The nearby San Diego River provided water for the settlement, and wild grapes and roses grew in the chaparrals. Plenty of game animals roamed the area. "It is a good country," he wrote in his diary. But soon the river dried up in the heat, which withered the plants. Little food was available, and the Spaniards sent a ship back to New Spain for supplies.

Captain Portolá headed north to explore Monterey, leaving behind some soldiers to protect the missionaries at San Diego. Father Serra, meanwhile, prepared to teach the Catholic faith to local Indians.

Communication between the Spaniards and the Native Americans was difficult because the groups spoke different languages. One result of the language problem was that the Spaniards renamed the nearby Yuman-speakers, calling them Diegueños, after the mission. The lack of communication also made it difficult for the Spaniards and Indians to trust and respect one another.

This hierro, *or branding iron, features the entwined letters* S *and* D. *The burned-in symbol, or brand, marked the livestock of San Diego de Alcalá.*

In 1769 Captain Gaspar de Portolá led a band of Spanish soldiers northward from New Spain (what is now Mexico) to San Diego in Alta California. Portolá later journeyed even farther north to the harbor at Monterey, which would become the capital of the 21-member mission chain.

The Yuman-speakers resented the missionaries for settling on Indian land without permission. Moreover, the Spaniards had made camp in a place where Indians harvested plants and roots. Native Americans took offense when the soldiers shot game animals that Indians counted on for food.

Tension and distrust among the groups quickly mounted. The Spaniards considered the Indians shameless for not wearing enough clothing. The Indians, who liked to keep clean and bathed almost daily, found the Spaniards dirty and smelly because they didn't wash often.

To befriend the Indians and to gain their trust, Father Serra offered them gifts of cloth and beads. The Native Americans hadn't seen cloth before and were very interested in it. The Indians accepted the gifts and later returned to the mission for more.

Sometimes the Indians took cloth and other goods without asking. No one knows for sure why they did this. Yuman-speakers had a strong tradition of freely sharing belongings with one another, so some experts believe that the Indians took items from the Spanish camp simply because their culture had different rules about personal ownership. Other people think that the Indians took things from the Spaniards to show their anger toward the newcomers. Whatever the reason, the behavior caused the Spaniards to view the Indians as thieves.

Trouble Brews

After weeks of tension and mistrust, the Native Americans revolted against the Spaniards. Armed with clubs and arrows, they surrounded the Spanish camp. But their weapons were no match for the soldiers' guns. The Indians killed one soldier and a servant before losing the battle. During the conflict, three Indians lost their lives, and many others were wounded. Afterward, a restless peace settled over Mission San Diego.

Father Serra was still determined to convert the Indians to Catholicism. He had befriended one young Indian boy, who was curious about the mission and had learned a few Spanish words. Father Serra soon convinced the boy to bring people from the Native American villages for baptism—the first step toward converting the Indians to the new religion.

In the baptismal ceremony, the priest would pour water over the head of the new church member to accept the person into the religious community. But the Indians probably did not realize that mission rules required baptized Indians to live at the mission and to practice the Catholic religion.

When local Indians brought a baby to San Diego de Alcalá to be baptized, Serra was overjoyed. It isn't clear why the Native Americans agreed to take part in this ceremony—perhaps they were trying to gain the favor of the Spaniards. But just as Father Serra was about to pour the water on the baby's head, one of the Yuman-speaking villagers snatched the child away and ran off.

An illustration from the 1800s depicts the early baptism of an Indian baby in California. The priests baptized the children to bring them into the Roman Catholic community. The Indians probably didn't understand what the ritual meant.

Ready to Give Up

Portolá and his men returned to San Diego in January 1770. The journey back to San Diego from Monterey had been terrible. Unable to find much food, the soldiers had decided to eat their mules. The men were disappointed to learn that Mission San Diego was still having trouble finding food. The ship that had been sent for supplies months earlier hadn't yet arrived, and mission crops had failed from lack of rain. The Spaniards at San Diego de Alcalá were starving.

Portolá ordered the missionaries to abandon San Diego de Alcalá if the supply ship didn't turn up by March 19. Serra pleaded with Portolá to change his mind. A lookout was posted to watch for the ship every day, but the vessel was nowhere in sight.

On the afternoon of March 19, the lookout shouted, "Sail ho!" Far in the distance, the supply ship's sails stood tall above the horizon. But instead of turning into the bay, the long-awaited craft kept sailing north and, before long, disappeared.

Portolá once again insisted that everyone abandon the mission. But Father Serra convinced the captain that the ship had been a sign that they should

stay. A few days later, the ship docked at San Diego, bringing food and supplies. The mission was saved.

Mission Life

The soldiers at Mission San Diego de Alcalá replaced the

ABOUT YUMAN-SPEAKERS, A SPANISH SOLDIER SAID, "THIS TRIBE IS THE MOST RESTLESS, STUBBORN, WARLIKE, AND HOSTILE TOWARD US, AND FULL OF THE SPIRIT OF INDEPENDENCE."

small huts with sturdier buildings made of wooden poles. In 1770 Father Serra felt San Diego de Alcalá was well established enough for him to leave

and set up more missions. Father Luís Jayme took Father Serra's place in San Diego.

Over the next few years, Indians came to the mission—mainly because they were ill from diseases that the Spaniards had unknowingly carried from Europe. When the shamans couldn't heal the sick, villagers went to the padres for help. The Indians thought that since the Spaniards had brought the diseases, they could also provide a cure. But in most cases, Native Americans who were ill eventually died.

Some Indians came to the mission for food. Several years with little rain had made the land dry and had killed plants on which Native Americans depended. But the priests, who were having trouble growing crops in the poor climate, also lacked food.

Native Americans who went to San Diego de Alcalá probably didn't realize that the priests

Baptized Indians, or neophytes, had to live and work at the missions. The Franciscans taught the neophytes to plow, to plant, and to harvest, as well as to herd livestock.

expected them to stay for good. Under the Franciscan mission system, Indians were supposed to live at the religious settlement and to abandon their age-old way of life. Mission Indians had to give up their own religion for the Catholic faith.

Another condition of joining the mission was that the Indians had to work there. The missionaries taught the neophytes to farm the land and to take care of livestock so that the mission would have food. This type of life attracted few Yuman-speakers, who were used to hunting and gathering.

The soldiers at the mission provided another problem for Native Americans. The soldiers abused the Indians—especially women. Indians who stood up to the Spaniards were harshly beaten. Many Yuman-speakers heard about this treatment and avoided the settlement. Father Jayme tried to solve the problem by asking the commander of the soldiers to discipline any men who hurt the Indians. But few soldiers actually were punished.

Father Jayme's solution was to move the mission away from the presidio. In 1774 the mission was relocated to a new site a few miles inland on the banks of the San Diego River. The priests hoped water from the river could be used to irrigate mission crops. An added benefit of this location was that the soil was more fertile for farming.

Over time the mission fields began to thrive and take up land. Yuman-speakers were left with less territory for hunting animals or harvesting roots and berries. The lack of food sources led more Indians to join the mission.

By 1774 the padres and neophytes had constructed many buildings at the new site. These structures sat around a large central, four-sided patio called a **quadrangle.** This quadrangle style was used at later missions in Alta California, too. Among the early structures at San Diego de Alcalá were a large wooden church, housing for the neophytes, a granary for storing grain, and living quarters for the priests.

More Conflict

With the soldiers out of the way, a few more Native Americans joined the mission. Like the other neophytes, these Indians had to attend religious services conducted in a language that was unfamiliar to them. Although they didn't understand the words or the meanings behind the Catholic ceremonies, the neophytes listened to the music and the chanting.

During the rituals, the priests sang and wore silk robes called vestments. The Yuman-speakers were familiar with the use of music and special clothing during ceremonies, since these things were part of their own

El Camino Reál

Mission San Juan Capistrano

Mission San Luis Rey de Francia

ALTA CALIFORNIA

Current Border

Monterey

Area of map

Mission San Diego de Alcalá

San Diego River

SAN DIEGO PRESIDIO

San Diego Bay

PACIFIC OCEAN

Miles
0 5 10 20

0 10 20
Kilometers

Highlights of the Southern Coast, early 1800s

BAJA CALIFORNIA

Current Border

Artistic neophytes at San Diego de Alcalá decorated mission buildings, such as this doorway overhang (above), with floral patterns and shell designs.

Yuman-speakers who hadn't joined the mission attacked it in 1775, as shown in this nineteenth-century picture (below). Wanting to force the Spaniards to leave, the Indians burned buildings and killed Father Luís Jayme, the priest in charge.

culture, too. A love for music and ritual were two things the Spaniards and the Indians shared and might explain in part why some of the Yuman-speakers agreed to join the mission.

Back in the Indian villages, the shamans and other leaders worried about the number of their people joining the Spanish settlement. The leaders, angry that the Spaniards were taking land and resources that villagers needed, also feared the Indian way of life would end. Intending to destroy the mission, the leaders sent messengers to find people who would be willing to fight the Spaniards.

At midnight on November 4, 1775, 800 Yuman-speakers crept up to the mission and set fire to the buildings. Father Jayme rushed out of the blaze and was beaten to death. Another padre escaped by shielding himself from the Indians' arrows with a pillow. Although the mission was within sight of the presidio, the guard on duty at the fort ignored the flames, and the soldiers slept through the night. San Diego de Alcalá was destroyed, but the missionaries didn't leave.

When word of the assault reached Father Serra, he was determined to found additional missions. Spanish officials, also in support of building more settlements, sent soldiers to fend off Indian attacks. In the year following the conflict, more Spanish soldiers came to San Diego de Alcalá to protect the mission.

By 1778 further unrest had occurred in the Indian communities outside the mission. Learning that Native American villagers were making arrows to use against the Spaniards, a group of soldiers killed two of the villagers and whipped many others.

Rebuilding

Despite the violence, the padres and neophytes continued work-

ing on the church and other structures. San Diego de Alcalá soon had a kitchen, a corral for horses, and a harness room to hold riding and farming equipment. The mission's fields produced crops of wheat and barley. Cattle, sheep, and goats grazed the pastures.

The mission also had a dormitory where Indian boys and men stayed. In these cramped quarters, illness again took hold, and the sickness spread to Indians outside the mission. Many local Native Americans died. As a result, the tribelets' shamans lost the chance to share their

After the rebellion of 1775, the missionaries and neophytes reestablished Mission San Diego. They constructed a bell wall (above left) to house five bells and built long corridors (left) that led to storerooms and living quarters.

37

healing methods and ceremonies with the next generation of Yuman-speakers. The Indians' traditional way of life was disappearing.

In 1797 a total of 565 Indians joined the mission, raising the population of San Diego de Alcalá higher than that of any other mission at the time. These neophytes, who mainly worked as farmers and ranchers, helped the priests make San Diego de Alcalá one of California's most productive missions.

Mission San Juan Capistrano

Mission San Juan Capistrano, located north of San Diego de Alcalá, was actually founded twice. The first time, Father Serra asked a fellow priest—Father Fermín Francisco de Lasuén—to choose a site. In 1775 Father Lasuén pounded a cross into the ground in what is now southern Orange County.

Shoshonean-speakers in the area quietly watched. When the Spaniards began building other structures, the Indians volunteered to help. They cut wood and reeds and carried them to the site. Later they helped hang the mission bells from a tree limb.

The group worked for eight days, until news arrived about the raid at San Diego de Alcalá. Greatly upset, Father Lasuén buried the mission bells to protect them and then hurried south to San Diego to help the priests there.

In 1776, after Mission San Diego was running again, Father Serra brought two priests and 22 soldiers to the mission site that Father Lasuén had abandoned earlier. They found the cross, then dug up the bells and rehung them from a tree. When the group began to

The design for the livestock brand of Mission San Juan Capistrano twists together the letters C, A, *and* P.

construct buildings, Shoshonean-speakers again assisted. The Spaniards renamed these Native Americans Juaneños, after the mission.

Soon afterward Father Serra brought a few neophytes from nearby Mission San Gabriel, which lay to the north of San Juan Capistrano. These Indians knew Shoshonean words and could act as interpreters. Their presence may have encouraged some Shoshonean-speakers to join the mission.

Within two years, about 150 neophytes were living and working at San Juan Capistrano. By 1784, 400 more Indians had joined. At this mission, as at others, the baptized Indians were required to remain at the mission, to work the land for no pay, and to attend church services.

Making Adobe

Priests and Indians from other missions taught the neophytes at San Juan Capistrano the skills needed for constructing buildings. With the neophytes as the main labor force, San Juan Capistrano became one of the most beautiful missions. The first permanent structure built at the site was a church called Serra's Chapel.

Instead of wood, the church was crafted from a material called *adobe*—a heavy clay soil common to dry regions. Few trees grew in southern Alta California, so wood wasn't readily available. The missionaries used lumber mainly for roof beams. To find adobe, however, all a worker had to do was look underfoot. As a result, adobe became the building blocks of San Juan Capistrano and other missions.

San Juan Capistrano was named for Saint John of Capistrano, an Italian lawyer and religious thinker who had lived during the 1300s. Because its buildings were so beautiful, San Juan Capistrano became known as the "Jewel of the Missions."

The priests taught the mission Indians to become experts at making adobe bricks. First, the neophytes dug up the clay, which they threw into a shallow ditch and covered with grass or straw. Then the Indians added water to make the mixture stick together. Workers, including children, stirred the materials with their feet.

Neophytes put the sticky adobe into wooden molds and placed them in the sun to dry. The clay hardened into bricks. Children guarded the drying clay to make sure that animals didn't make tracks in the soft material. Dried adobe bricks were large and weighed about 60 pounds each.

Building Missions

The padres showed the Indians where to build the mission structures. Some of the priests had measuring sticks to make sure the walls were straight and of the same length. Other padres just walked along the site in a rectangular path, pointing out where the mission walls should go. Walls planned in this way were often crooked.

Constructing a mission was hard work, and the Indians did most of the labor. First they collected stones for the building's foundation. The stones were stacked to create the base of a building. Indian workers applied mortar to make the rocks stick together. The mortar was made from limestone melted in a special oven called a kiln.

Next the workers stacked the heavy adobe bricks to build walls. The thick adobe walls helped the buildings stay cool in summer. The walls also held in

The walls of old living quarters at San Juan Capistrano show the stacked adobe bricks used in the mission's construction.

Curved clay roof tiles lean against a cone-shaped kiln (oven). The neophytes molded sheets of wet clay into the desired shape and then dried them in the kiln. The tiles protected the adobe walls from water damage.

heat created by small fireplaces, which kept the buildings warm in winter.

Because adobe turns to mud when it gets wet, the missions needed a solid roof to keep rain off the walls and to prevent the buildings from crumbling. The neophytes covered the roofs with curved tiles made from thin sheets of kiln-dried clay.

Then the Indians white-washed the mission walls with a mixture of lime, salt, and sometimes goat's milk.

The workers constructed San Juan Capistrano's buildings around a quadrangle. This enclosed layout provided a defense from possible attacks. It also allowed the priests to keep track of the neophytes.

Other California missions followed a similar building plan, with the church usually forming one wall of the quadrangle. The priests' rooms made up another side of the rectangle. At the back of the quadrangle sat *monjerios,* or separate quarters where girls and unmarried women stayed. Each mission also included workshops, classrooms, storage rooms, and kitchens.

As the number of people living at the missions increased, so did the number of buildings. Some structures, such as the boys' quarters, often stood outside the quadrangle's walls. Small Indian villages—for neophytes who were married—also sat beyond the quadrangle.

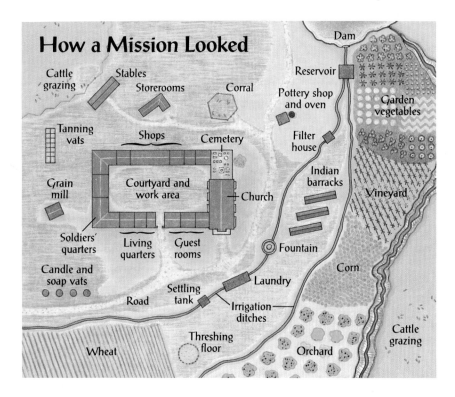

How a Mission Looked

Cattle grazing · Stables · Storerooms · Corral · Dam · Reservoir · Pottery shop and oven · Garden vegetables · Tanning vats · Shops · Cemetery · Filter house · Grain mill · Courtyard and work area · Church · Indian barracks · Vineyard · Soldiers' quarters · Living quarters · Guest rooms · Fountain · Corn · Candle and soap vats · Laundry · Cattle grazing · Road · Settling tank · Irrigation ditches · Wheat · Threshing floor · Orchard

Each of California's 21 missions was slightly different, but all had common elements. This artwork shows how a mission and its lands were typically arranged. Because supplies from New Spain rarely arrived, the missions became self-sufficient. Priests set aside land for livestock and crops. Local water supplies were harnessed to provide water for washing, cooking, and irrigation. At workshops both within and beyond the main mission buildings, neophytes ground wheat into flour, pressed olives and grapes, refined livestock hides into leather, and made soap and candles from tallow (animal fat). As the mission's main workforce, the neophytes received food, clothing, and shelter in exchange for their labor.

A New Church

By the late 1700s, the padres at San Juan Capistrano had decided that Serra's Chapel was too small to seat the 700 neophytes who were living at the mission. Father Vicente Fuster and Father Norberto de Santiago, the priests in charge then, wanted to build the grandest church ever seen in Alta California. Instead of adobe, this church would be made of stone.

In the spring of 1797, workers laid the first stone. The priests' plan called for a huge, cross-shaped building nearly 150 feet long (about half the length of a modern football field). The padres wanted the church ceiling to be arched with seven domes. They imagined a magnificent tower so tall it could be spotted 10 miles away.

The neophytes gathered sandstone from two nearby quarries, or rock pits. This was hard labor.

The Indians loaded large stones into carts that were hauled by oxen. Sometimes the workers themselves dragged the stones with chains. Women and children carried smaller rocks in nets across their backs.

But the padres and the neophytes at San Juan Capistrano weren't skilled stoneworkers. Instead of cutting the stones into blocks and stacking them like bricks, the workers used the rough-shaped rocks hauled from the quarry. They simply fitted the stones side by side and sealed the leftover spaces with mortar.

To make sure the building was durable and attractive, the priests hired Isídro Aguilár, a skilled stonemason from New Spain. In 1799 Aguilár arrived to guide the workers. He showed them his trade and carved elegant stone doorways and arches for the church.

Work slowed during the early 1800s. A drought (a long period with no rain) ruined the mission's crops. Lacking food, the people got sick. Many died, including Father Fuster. A fire later destroyed food kept in one of the storehouses, and, in 1803, Aguilár died.

But the work of building the church continued. Three years later, the labor was finished. San Juan Capistrano's new

An old painting depicts the Great Stone Church as it looked before being damaged by an earthquake in 1812.

church could seat more than 1,000 neophytes. The bells ringing in its high tower could be heard for miles.

The Spaniards were delighted with the completed structure, which they called the Great Stone Church. They invited priests, neophytes, and soldiers from other missions to admire the fine new building at Mission

A thriving community in the early 1800s, San Juan Capistrano had an outdoor kitchen area (above) with several ovens usable at one time. Colorful flowers (top) nearly hide one of the mission's bell towers.

A young boy accidentally started the fire that destroyed San Juan Capistrano's storehouse in the early 1800s. He had gone into the building for goods but then began chasing bats and dropped the candle he was carrying. The boy escaped the flames, but the building was left in ruins.

San Juan Capistrano and celebrated with them for three days.

The Mission Crumbles

In 1812 San Juan Capistrano was thriving. Its quadrangle had busy soap and candle factories, a blacksmith shop, a winery and wine cellar, spinning and weaving rooms, and even a hat shop.

The quake of December 1812 caused the roof of the Great Stone Church to collapse inward. Church services were in progress when the disaster occurred, and many neophytes were killed. Within less than a year, the mission's records—usually so full of good news and reports of new building projects— read only, "nothing worthy of note has been done."

The mission had an olive press to make oil, two huge granaries, and a tannery for tanning animal hides. San Juan Capistrano also operated a foundry for casting metal—the only one in the mission chain.

Major crops grown at the mission included wheat, corn, and beans. Fruit orchards produced peaches and apricots. Livestock such as cattle, sheep, and goats grazed the pastures. Horses and mules roamed the grounds. San Juan Capistrano regularly traded many of its farm goods with other Spanish missions.

On the morning of December 8, 1812, a major earthquake struck San Juan Capistrano during early church services. The tower shook and crashed down on the arched roof of the church, caving it in. Nearly 40 neophytes died, including two young bell ringers who fell from the tower. The priests, who were in the front of the church at the time, survived.

After the rubble had been cleared away, what remained of the stone church was full of cracks. The padres held church services in Serra's Chapel once again. No one had the heart to rebuild the Great Stone Church.

During the following year, neophytes spent time repairing the damage to other mission buildings. But when disease struck, many Indians died. With fewer workers and the loss of the Great Stone Church, San Juan Capistrano began to decline.

Mission San Luis Rey de Francia

In 1784, after having founded nine missions, Father Serra died. Father Lasuén replaced Father Serra as head of the mission system. Part of Father Lasuén's new role was to found several more religious settlements. In 1798 he chose to locate California's eighteenth mission halfway between San Diego de Alcalá and San Juan Capistrano.

The spot was in a broad valley, which early priests had described as so green that it seemed as if it had been planted. Fresh water flowed from the nearby San Luis Rey River and from several underground springs. Father Lasuén wrote that the local Shoshonean-speakers (called Luiseños by the Spaniards) greeted him kindly and welcomed the Spanish newcomers.

But the Indians tell quite a different story. According to the Native Americans, their chief told the priests to go away. The Indian leader later received gifts from the missionaries, however, and eventually came to accept the Spaniards. Within two months, the mission had 214 neophytes.

The brand of San Luis Rey de Francia looks like the number five.

Father Peyri

San Luis Rey de Francia's main priest was Father Antonio Peyri, who stayed at Mission San Luis Rey for 33 years. Under Father Peyri's long-term direction, the mission flourished.

Peyri modeled the mission chapel after the Great Stone Church at San Juan Capistrano. But Mission San Luis Rey de Francia's chapel was built from adobe. Sitting on a hill, San Luis Rey de Francia's cross-shaped church could hold about 1,000 worshipers. The mission quadrangle, which was bigger than a modern football field, overlooked fruit trees and grain crops. A French visitor once commented that Mission San Luis Rey looked like a palace.

Father Peyri oversaw many projects at the mission and dreamed up new ones. One of his ideas was to conserve water by making what he called a *lavandería*. The lavandería, or laundry area, sat in a shallow

Mission San Luis Rey de Francia was named after King Louis IX of France, whose enthusiasm for fighting religious wars in the Middle East gained him sainthood in 1297. The mission became very successful, partly because it was run by the same priest—Father Antonio Peyri (inset)—for more than 30 years.

Among Father Peyri's many projects was San Luis Rey's lavandería (laundry area). Water flowed beside stone steps (left), through a spout, and into a pool (bottom left). After being used for washing clothes, the dirty water passed through a filter (below) before being channeled into the mission's gardens.

valley in front of the mission. Water from a spring flowed down both sides of a long, wide stairway that neophytes had built, then gurgled out of two carved stone heads at the base of the steps.

The water collected in two brick-lined ponds. Here Indian women bathed daily and did the laundry each Saturday, beating clothes on the stairs to get them clean. The dirty water drained from the ponds, passing through

Pablo Tac

Much of what is known about the neophytes at San Luis Rey de Francia came from a mission Indian named Pablo Tac. Tac was born at the mission in 1822. A good student, he was chosen to accompany Father Peyri to Italy at the age of 10 and went to school there. While in Europe, Tac wrote about how Indian life had changed since the arrival of the Spaniards. His account survived long after he did. Like thousands of other mission Indians exposed to European illnesses, Tac didn't live a long life. He died a month before turning 20.

Pablo Tac not only wrote about life at Mission San Luis Rey, he also drew pictures of Native American customs, including ceremonial dances.

a filter that caught the dirt and soap. The clean water then flowed directly into a nearby vegetable and fruit garden. Because of the lavandería, precious water was used for many purposes instead of being wasted.

Daily Life

The neophytes at Mission San Luis Rey, as well as at other missions, had to adjust to a life that centered around prayer and work. The ringing of the bells signaled the start of each day. Although the padres loved the routine, the Indians preferred following the natural rhythms of the sun, moon, and seasons.

Bells at sunrise called the neophytes to morning church services. In the church, the Indians sat on the cool tiled floor. Men worshiped on one side of the building and women on the other. From a tiny pulpit sticking out of the left wall, Father Peyri led the prayers.

In church and during classes, the Indians learned the Catholic faith. Many of the neophytes just memorized the words and repeated them when the priests said to do so. The Indians probably didn't understand the purpose of the Catholic rituals. Many secretly practiced their traditional religious ceremonies when they had the chance.

After morning prayers, the bells rang again and everyone went to breakfast. The neophytes usually ate *atole,* a rich grain gruel. An hour later, bells sent the neophytes to work.

The mission Indians worked hard all day. In the workshops, neophytes made shoes, wove cloth, pressed oil from olives, and molded adobe bricks. Many Indians labored in the fields, plowing, planting, or harvesting. Others branded cattle, sheared sheep, or milked cows. During work hours, young boys kept animals away from the crops, while girls were taught to weave.

The noon bells signaled lunch. Some neophytes chose to eat in the mission kitchen, while others went to their homes just outside the mission walls. The Indians sometimes ate tortillas or *pozole,* a stew with meat and vegetables. After lunch came *siesta,*

Neophytes at San Luis Rey decorated this holy water basin with geometric designs. Before church services, people dipped their right hands in the water and made a sign of the cross.

when everyone rested for two hours before going back to work.

Many mission Indians found it frustrating to conform to this rigid schedule. Sometimes neophytes wouldn't show up for work or would sit down on the job. Others simply ran away from the missions.

The padres and soldiers punished neophytes who didn't follow the rules. Many Indians were whipped. Runaways were hunted down by Spanish soldiers, beaten, and taken back to the mission. Indians who ran away more than once had their ankles chained together for several days as a form of discipline.

At San Luis Rey de Francia, Father Peyri showed concern for the neophytes, and the Indians generally respected him. Once, when an assistant padre mistreated an Indian, Peyri asked the priest to leave. To help keep order at the mission, which was housing 1,500 neophytes by 1810, Peyri used neophytes as *alcaldes,* or overseers. The job of the overseers was to supervise the neophyte workers and to help manage the Indian community. Other missions came to use the same system.

Mission Trade

With its varied economic activities, Mission San Luis Rey produced many of the goods that the padres, soldiers, and neophytes required for survival. Items that couldn't be made at the mission were often obtained through trade. For example, the priests needed buttons, iron tools, needles, and books, as well as candleholders and musical instruments for church services.

Father Peyri got many of these desired goods from non-Spanish trade ships that sailed up and down the coast loaded with useful supplies. Spain had forbidden the missionaries from trading with other countries because Spain wanted to prevent

Father Peyri regularly traded with foreign merchants. Using mission goods, he was able to barter for items that San Luis Rey didn't produce.

foreigners from setting foot in Alta California. But to keep the missions going, the priests found it necessary to break the Spanish Empire's rules.

When foreign ships arrived near Mission San Luis Rey, Father Peyri went on board and visited the trading rooms. Set up like stores, the rooms had all sorts of goods. The priest chose what he needed and paid for the items with mission products, such as tallow (animal fat used for making candles) and cowhides. In fact, so many hides were traded that they later

became known as "California dollars."

With supplies from the trading ships, San Luis Rey de Francia had all it needed to support its people and to help some of the less productive missions. During the late 1820s, San Luis Rey was thriving. The mission owned 28,000 sheep, 22,000 cattle, and 1,500 horses.

Peyri had many plans for the mission. Political changes taking place in Alta California during the 1820s, however, made him realize that most of his projects would never get off the ground.

51

PART THREE

Secularization of the Missions

THE EARLY 1800s MARKED A TIME OF TROUBLE FOR Spain. Fighting a war in Europe, the nation was strapped for money. Spain had little to spare for its settlements in Alta California.

The Franciscan priests no longer relied on New Spain for supplies. Instead the missions depended mainly on goods produced by the neophytes. The padres traded fruits, vegetables, leather goods, soap, and tallow among the missions.

By this time, the missions were also providing goods to soldiers living near the settlements. The soldiers weren't the only ones who

By the early 1820s, San Luis Rey de Francia was one of the largest missions. It covered roughly six acres of land.

received such provisions. Settlers who resided in growing pueblos near the missions also got their supplies from the Franciscans.

The settlers and soldiers were frustrated by Spain's economic and political problems. Short of money and agricultural goods, these people hungered for the thriving orchards, fields, and pastures of the missions. The settlers and soldiers grew angry that most of Alta California's fertile land was in the hands of the Franciscan priests.

New Threats

In 1813 Spain passed a law limiting the power of the mission priests. The law ordered the Franciscans at missions more than 10 years old to transfer their authority to a bishop appointed by Spain. But the ruling wasn't actually made known in Alta California, and mission life remained much the same. In 1821 New Spain reenacted the 1813 decree. The bishop, occupied with other church business, still allowed the settlements to stay under the control of the Franciscan priests.

FATHER LASUÉN DECLARED IN THE EARLY 1800S THAT, "THE [SPANISH] GOVERNMENT IS CONTRIBUTING NOTHING . . . EVERYTHING [COMES FROM] THE MISSIONS, THE MISSIONARIES, AND THE INDIANS."

The year 1821 also saw New Spain win its independence from the Spanish Empire. New Spain soon became known as the Republic of Mexico. Among the territories claimed by Mexico was Alta California. Mexico then began drafting a constitution (a set of laws) to guarantee personal freedom for all individuals—including Indians.

Settlers who lived near the missions saw this political change as a chance to take control of mission land. These people, called Californios, were mainly of Spanish heritage but also included newcomers with American or Mexican backgrounds. The Californios had long wanted better land on which to run their ranches.

Californios argued that the mission system was a failure because most neophytes hadn't yet fully adopted Spanish ways. In reality many Californios disliked the mission system because they wanted to take the mission land and property for themselves.

Throughout the 1820s, disputes arose between the Californios and the missionaries. Hoping to acquire mission land, Californios urged secularization—a policy that would remove the missions from Franciscan control. People in favor of secularization wanted the government to divide mission land into estates that private citizens would then be allowed to own. Secularization would also give Indians freedom to leave the missions.

The idea of secularization had been around for many years. In fact, Spain had always intended that the Indians would one day take over the missions. According to the original mission plan, the Franciscans were simply holding the missions in trust until the time when Native Americans would be ready to manage the buildings and the land themselves.

The padres, however, argued that the neophytes weren't yet ready for secularization. The Franciscans claimed that the neophytes still needed the benefit of the routines and supervision offered by mission life. The priests also feared that, without the missions, neophytes would

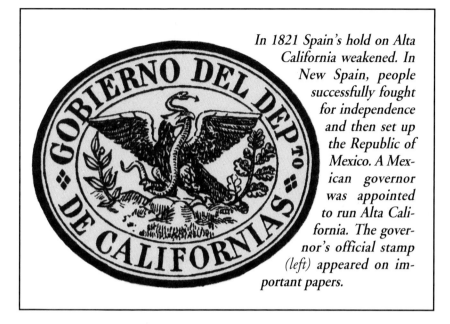

In 1821 Spain's hold on Alta California weakened. In New Spain, people successfully fought for independence and then set up the Republic of Mexico. A Mexican governor was appointed to run Alta California. The governor's official stamp (left) appeared on important papers.

give up the Catholic religion and forget Spanish ways. Moreover, the padres suspected that the Californios—not the Indians—would gain control of mission land once secularization laws took effect.

Despite the protests of the priests, secularization proceeded as planned. The Franciscans, losing their authority, could no longer run the missions with a free hand. The Mexican government appointed civil administrators to oversee the mission lands and Indians.

Life at the Missions

Although Mexico allowed the mission churches to continue to hold services, the government intended to replace the Franciscans with Mexican priests. Many of the Franciscans had to return to Spain or find other missionary work in Alta California. Some Spanish padres stayed at the missions because few Mexican priests were actually available to replace them.

At Mission San Luis Rey, Father Peyri feared that secularization would deprive the Indians of mission land and livestock. He argued with Mexican officials not to secularize San Luis Rey de Francia. When officials refused to listen, Father Peyri felt defeated.

Late one night in January of 1832, Father Peyri left the mission in secret, fearing that the neophytes might try to convince him to stay. Hearing that the padre had left, about 500 Indians from Mission San Luis Rey rushed to San Diego, where Father Peyri's ship was setting sail. They arrived just in time to see the priest waving good-bye. A year later, Mexico began to secularize San Luis Rey de Francia.

Mission San Juan Capistrano also was secularized in 1833. The neophytes received some of

A drawing from the late 1800s shows Father Peyri on deck as his ship pulls away from the coast in 1832. At that time, Mexican authorities had decided to secularize the missions—that is, to transfer them from the Roman Catholic Church to private owners. Peyri opposed the policy because he thought it would treat the Indians unfairly, but he got nowhere. Feeling utterly defeated, he chose to return to his native Spain rather than watch Mission San Luis Rey be broken apart.

the mission land, but most of the property was granted to Californios. A few Franciscan missionaries stayed at the mission and tried to keep it running. But without workers, the mission quickly fell into ruin. The neglected crops, orchards, and livestock wasted away.

In 1834 San Diego de Alcalá was secularized. The Mexican governor of Alta California, José Figueroa, told the neophytes in person that they were now free. He viewed the mission Indians as new Mexican citizens who no longer were under Franciscan authority. The governor offered Indians at San Diego de Alcalá plots of mission land that had enough room for a home and a cattle pasture.

But only 2 out of 59 of these Indian families accepted the offer. Some Native Americans at San Diego de Alcalá decided to stay with the priests. Others wanted to live in Indian communities as free individuals.

Secularization laws freed the neophytes from having to stay on mission lands. But most former mission Indians had no link with their age-old ways. Many Indians, such as this group on the outskirts of the town of San Diego, had a hard time making a living. Unused to being free, some Native Americans gambled away their land, tools, and clothing and ended up in poverty.

Very few wanted to become Mexican citizens. As a result, much of Mission San Diego's land went to Californios.

After the Californios got land from San Diego de Alcalá, San Juan Capistrano, and San Luis Rey de Francia, they set up large, private estates called ranchos. Wanting even more ranchland, the Californios persuaded Indians to sell the farms and pastures acquired after secular-ization. Some Californios found it easy to cheat former neophytes, most of whom had never been taught to read and were unfamiliar with Mexican laws of landownership.

Civil Administrators

Throughout the late 1830s and the 1840s, civil administrators were appointed to oversee what had once been mission land.

In this nineteenth-century drawing, Pablo de la Portilla (on horseback), the civil administrator of Mission San Luis Rey in 1833, urges the newly freed labor force to return to work. The ex-neophytes refused to obey him. By 1843 the once-thriving mission was unable to support itself.

These administrators were generally greedy, power hungry, and dishonest. They forced Native Americans who had remained at the missions to become laborers for little or no pay. The civil administrators also beat the Indians or sent them to friends to work as unpaid laborers.

The administrators abused mission property during their rule and gave away land that had once belonged to the missions. One of Mission San Luis Rey's managers even took plates and glasses from the dining room, and another administrator sold tiles that had once covered the mission's roof.

Pío Pico

At the height of his wealth, Pío Pico held thousands of acres of land.

Julio César

Panning for gold was one of the jobs that Julio César took after leaving San Luis Rey.

Pío Pico, a Californio, was born at Mission San Gabriel in 1801. He grew up in San Diego and managed a store for a time. Pico later got involved in politics and briefly served as governor after overthrowing the previous officeholder in 1831.

Pico was named administrator of San Luis Rey de Francia around 1835. Like many Californios, Pico gained much land and wealth after secularization. In fact, Pío Pico obtained a 133,400 acre rancho that had once belonged to nearby Mission San Juan Capistrano. The rancho was so large that Pico, it was said, could ride on horseback all day long without ever leaving his land.

In 1845 Pico again became governor. He ordered that all of the mission buildings be sold or rented. Then he freely offered mission property to his friends and relatives. Pico eventually lost most of his vast lands, however, to U.S. settlers in the 1880s.

Julio César, a neophyte, was born around 1824 at San Luis Rey de Francia. He described the mission as "very rich" with herds of cattle and goats and fields of wheat and corn.

After secularization Mission San Luis Rey was run by various civil administrators, including Pío Pico. César worked in the fields for the administrators. A good singer, he was often asked to sing mass. But he only received food and clothing—not money—for his work. César used these words to describe life under the rule of the overseers: "[We] were at the mercy of the administrator, who ordered the beatings whenever and how many he felt like."

As Mission San Luis Rey began to fall into ruin, César moved on. For the rest of his life, he worked odd jobs throughout California and in Mexico, loading ships, carrying water, mining gold, and breaking horses.

With the administrators in charge, few Indian families could make a successful living. Most ex-neophytes were forced to work as laborers on Californio ranchos or else couldn't find work at all.

Some of the Shoshonean- and Yuman-speakers fled inland to get away from the Californios. Here the ex-neophytes came in contact with nonmission Indians, who had long objected to settlers taking over Indian land. Hoping to drive away the Californios, these groups staged numerous raids to steal cattle and horses from the ranchos.

Indians and Californios alike were killed during the raids, and in some cases the raiders took hostages. In 1837, for example, Indians abducted two Californio girls from a rancho east of San Diego, and the girls were never seen again. But, despite the attacks, the ranchos grew under the leadership of a few wealthy Californio families.

Meanwhile, Indians became poorer. In 1839 an elderly Indian from San Juan Capistrano traveled northward all the way to Monterey, the capital of California. Troubled by what was happening to his people, the old man

AFTER SECULARIZA-TION, AN ELDERLY EX-NEOPHYTE REPORTED HARSH CONDITIONS TO THE GOVERNOR AND ADDED, "YOU CAN ORDER ME TO BE SHOT OR GIVE ME LIBERTY."

met with the governor, saying, "I am not an animal that they may make me work for masters who are not to my liking." His words convinced officials to forbid the civil administrators from hiring out Indians to their friends as laborers.

Nevertheless, Indians remained the main workforce on the ranchos. They herded and slaughtered cattle and cooked and served food in Californio homes. The lifeways of their ancestors were a thing of the past. Without traditional communities to sustain them, many Indians gave in to the crushing burden of poverty and disease.

By 1844 the mission buildings along the southern coast of Alta California were beginning to crumble. People had bought or stolen the roof tiles, and the adobe walls had begun to melt back into mud. Soon afterward Pío Pico became the territory's governor and decided that all the missions must be sold or rented. He sold San Juan Capistrano to his brother-in-law and granted San Luis Rey de Francia to other relatives. An acquaintance bought San Diego de Alcalá.

The decline of the missions affected the territory's economy because the missions had long

Ex-neophytes often ended up working for the people who'd taken over mission lands. This young man was a zanjero. His job was to clear a rancho's irrigation ditches.

produced most trade items in Alta California. The settlements had supplied one another with fruits, vegetables, and wine and had manufactured hides and tallow to exchange for foreign-made goods. Without mission labor, fewer items were made locally and trade slowed.

The ranchos, which mainly raised beef cattle for hides, relied on outside suppliers for most other goods. The bulk of their trade was with U.S. merchants, who came and went freely in Alta California. Many of the U.S. traders who worked the territory eventually made their homes there.

U.S. Takeover

Aware of the region's economic potential, the U.S. government had long wanted to own the rich land of Alta California. In fact, the United States offered to purchase the region from Mexico in the early 1840s, but the Mexican government refused the bid.

For several years, disputes raged between the U.S. and Mexican governments over Alta California and other territories. In 1846 the United States declared war on Mexico. That year a U.S. force captured Monterey. Mexico

lost the conflict in 1848. Within two years, the U.S. government had made the region a state.

Soon people from the eastern United States headed to California to start new lives. Seeking

From 1846 to 1848, Mexico battled U.S. forces. Mexico lost the war and gave up Alta California to the United States as part of the peace agreement. The newly acquired territory later became the state of California.

A photograph from the late nineteenth century shows a woman whose family was born at San Juan Capistrano. She grinds grain in the traditional way, while nearby her husband chops wood.

land, these newcomers eyed the ranchos. In the early 1850s, the U.S. Congress passed new legislation that required Californios to produce proof in U.S. courts that they owned their estates. Unable to pay the huge legal costs involved, many Californios lost their property to U.S. settlers.

At about the same time, government officials ruled that Indians would also have to justify their land claims to the courts. But Native Americans were never told about this law. When no Indians presented claims, officials decided that white settlers could buy Native American lands. As a result, many Indian groups were left homeless.

Other legislation worked against Native Americans in California as well. One law stated that Indians couldn't testify against a white person in court. Another ruling declared that Native Americans could be arrested and hired out as laborers to anyone who posted bail. These laws were designed to make sure that the ranchos always had enough Indian laborers available.

Eventually, the U.S. government moved many Native Americans onto **reservations** (public land set aside for Indians). Reservations in southern California were usually located on rocky land that no one else wanted because it was difficult to farm. The Indians had trouble hunting and planting in these areas and came to rely on government funds and supplies to support their families.

Mission Buildings

By the late 1850s, U.S. settlers had claimed most of the ranchos in California. Meanwhile, the mission buildings, fields, orchards, and vineyards were in poor shape. People had stolen candlesticks, crosses, roof tiles, and adobe bricks from the churches and other structures. The once thriving crops had died from neglect.

For a few years, the crumbling buildings of San Luis Rey de Francia and San Diego de Alcalá housed members of the U.S. Army. The soldiers at Mission San Luis Rey tore down the church altar and stole some religious artifacts. At Mission San Diego, the soldiers built a second floor inside the church for their own quarters and stabled their horses on the first floor. Farther north, at Mission San Juan Capistrano, Serra's Chapel was used for storing hay.

The U.S. government returned the churches and some of the mission land to the Roman Catholic Church in the 1850s and the 1860s. New priests went to rebuild the missions but had little money to complete the task. Some mission priests rented out the buildings to schools and the army to make money. Nevertheless, by the late 1880s, the mission buildings in southern California were falling apart.

The U.S. government wasn't sure what to do with the missions. The U.S. Army quartered some of its forces in a few of the old churches. Other buildings were used as schools and storage areas. The government had returned the southern coast missions to the Church by the 1860s. But by then the buildings were in rough shape. The exposed adobe had slowly worn away at San Diego de Alcalá (top). The stone of San Luis Rey's garden gate (right) was crumbling. Broken-down arches at San Juan Capistrano (below) gave a view of the ruins of Serra's Chapel.

PART FOUR

The Missions in Modern Times

THE MISSIONS MIGHT HAVE STAYED IN RUINS HAD IT not been for the work of a few artists and writers. But in the late 1800s, paintings and photos that showed the haunting beauty of the mission remains attracted public interest. In 1884 author Helen Hunt Jackson published *Ramona*—a novel about early California— and people throughout the country were drawn by the dramatic history of the California missions.

Born in England in 1838, the artist Edwin Deakin eventually moved to California, where he became fascinated by the damaged mission buildings. He painted each of the 21 missions, including the remains of the Great Stone Church at San Juan Capistrano (left). By making the missions look neglected and mysterious, he spurred people to try to restore them.

In the 1880s, writer Helen Hunt Jackson wanted to make people aware of the hardships faced by the Indians in California. But, instead of inspiring people to help the Indians, her book Ramona *drew tourists to the missions.*

In 1895, to save the missions and other historic landmarks in California, writer and editor Charles F. Lummis started an organization called the Landmarks Club. It raised money to reconstruct buildings of historical importance.

San Juan Capistrano

The first project of the Landmarks Club was restoring San Juan Capistrano. The club put a new roof on fragile Serra's Chapel. With steel beams and cement, the workers strengthened the walls of the broken-down Great Stone Church. Their efforts sometimes backfired, however. When workers used gunpowder to clear some of the stone rubble near the church, for example, they accidentally blew up part of the remaining building.

In 1917, after fixing up several other missions, the Landmarks Club stopped its efforts. Catholic priests then took on the job of restoration. They worked to rebuild and preserve old mission structures.

Mission San Juan Capistrano was further rescued from decline by Father John O'Sullivan, a frail, young priest with tuberculosis who had visited the site in 1910. Drawn by the mission's history and beauty, he got permission from the Roman Catholic Church to restore the mission so it could hold services once again. But life in a crumbling mission wasn't comfortable. The buildings were so full of fleas that Father O'Sullivan had to sleep in a tent.

As the priest began to recover from his illness, he started to restore the mission with his own hands. He read about the building techniques that the neophytes had once used and decided to adopt this style.

Dressed in an outfit that a vaquero, or cowhand, might wear, Charles F. Lummis, the founder of the Landmarks Club, mounts his horse.

The Landmarks Club took on a big job at San Juan Capistrano. Serra's Chapel was near collapse *(left)* before renovation but looked fairly solid after a new roof was added *(below left)*. Father John O'Sullivan *(pictured in San Juan Capistrano's courtyard)* took over when the Landmarks Club stopped funding the repairs. By 1918 church services were again being held at the mission.

Father O'Sullivan sought out nearby families who owned bits of the original mission, including nails and roof tiles. To pay for such items and for the re-

By the 1950s, after many years of use as a religious college, Mission San Luis Rey was in fairly good shape.

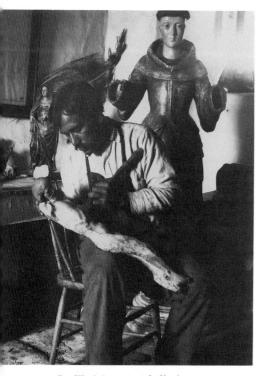

L. T. Meza, a skilled carpenter as well as a descendant of neophytes who'd built San Juan Capistrano, mended a statue during the mission's restoration.

building, he charged visitors a fee to tour the mission. He soon earned enough money to hire workers to help him with the restoration.

The priest painted the church walls and gathered religious artifacts from Spain. By 1918 O'Sullivan had turned dusty, owl-haunted Serra's Chapel back into an active church. Mission San Juan Capistrano once again had regular services and worshipers.

San Luis Rey de Francia

Like San Juan Capistrano, Mission San Luis Rey was uninhab-

ited and crumbling. But in 1892, a group of Mexican priests was looking for a place to start a seminary (a school for priests). Catholic leaders let the men use the buildings at San Luis Rey de Francia and put Father Joseph O'Keefe, an American, in charge.

Even though they weren't trained builders, Father O'Keefe and the other priests reroofed the church and repaired its cracked dome so services could be held. In 1903 the Mexican priests went back home, but Father O'Keefe stayed on to expand the seminary.

He began to rebuild the quadrangle but didn't follow the plan of the original structure. Using adobe bricks saved from the ruins, he made two-storied buildings around the old mission patio. Although the new quadrangle wasn't as big as the old one had been, Father O'Keefe used stronger materials so that the structures would last.

From the 1930s to the 1950s, the seminary's students and professors spent their spare time uncovering more ruins. Guided by the writings of Pablo Tac—a neophyte boy from Mission San Luis Rey—the excavators found Father Peyri's lavandería. Beneath layers of mud in a swamp, the workers discovered the old stone water spouts that had once overhung the brick pools.

The excavations also revealed two huge kilns that the neophtyes had once used for drying and heating tiles. The larger kiln was 15 feet wide and 20 feet deep. Workers continue to uncover and restore the remains at San Luis Rey de Francia, which now serves as a retreat center for religious groups.

San Diego de Alcalá

At Mission San Diego, heavy restoration didn't begin until 1931. Years earlier, the U.S. Army had torn down many of the buildings because they were unsafe. For a while, the remaining structures housed a school for Indian children.

People in the city of San Diego raised money to restore the church and other buildings. After retrieving the mission's bells from the backyard of an old Californio home where they had been stored, workers

In 1912 travelers taking part in the "Home of Ramona" tour visited the missions of southern California, including San Diego de Alcalá.

rehung them in the new *campanario* (bell wall). Trees and a garden were planted on the mission grounds.

By the late 1980s, San Diego de Alcalá was an active church with a congregation of 1,750 families. Some church members were descendants of neophytes. The growing congregation needed more seating room, so the Roman Catholic Church decided to build a new meeting hall along part of the quadrangle. Experts thought an old Indian cemetery lay beneath the proposed site, however. Indians and other people in San Diego were outraged that the meeting hall would be built on ground that many Native Americans considered sacred.

Angry community members delayed the building plans for a year, but the Catholic Church went ahead with the work. Yet in 1988, when workers started digging, they came across Indian bones and artifacts and realized the site was actually a mass burial ground of Indians. Local Native Americans staged a number of protests to stop the project.

Because of the conflict, the Catholic Church agreed in 1989

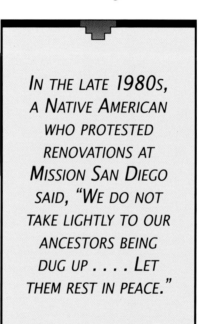

IN THE LATE *1980s,* A NATIVE AMERICAN WHO PROTESTED RENOVATIONS AT MISSION SAN DIEGO SAID, "WE DO NOT TAKE LIGHTLY TO OUR ANCESTORS BEING DUG UP . . . . LET THEM REST IN PEACE."

to set aside part of the quadrangle as a private Indian burial ground. The Native Americans reburied the bones and artifacts, and the meeting hall was constructed elsewhere on the mission grounds.

The Southern Coast Missions Today

Once an isolated outpost surrounded by chaparrals, San Diego de Alcalá now sits in the busy port city of San Diego. The mission itself is a peaceful place. A stretch of grass surrounded by stately old trees marks the new Indian cemetery. Lush gardens filled with geraniums and exotic plants grow where the Spanish priests once grew crops.

At San Luis Rey de Francia, now in the town of Oceanside, tourists can walk down the steep steps of the old lavandería. The mission museum displays Father Peyri's rose-colored vestments. Thick adobe walls echo the conversations of visitors.

Mission San Juan Capistrano lies in a small town of the same name. Residents of the town are very involved in the continued restoration of the mission. They built a new church using the plans of the original Great Stone Church, whose ruins stand in front of the quadrangle.

Visitors to San Juan Capistrano can see for themselves that the mission walls aren't the same length because the priest who planned them didn't have a measuring stick. Tourists also view the tanning vats, where neophytes processed thousands of cowhides.

People who visit San Juan Capistrano during spring can see cliff swallows nesting under the eaves of the restored buildings. A legend says these small birds return to the mission each year on March 19—and every spring, the birds actually do reach the mission right around that time.

A small marker at San Diego de Alcalá honors Indians buried at the mission.

In the late 1980s, the idea of making Father Serra a saint drew strong reactions—including graffiti—from some people in southern California.

The three southern coast missions are now busy churches, as well as living museums. The old ranchos are a piece of California's distant history, however. The estates have been covered with new houses or broken into smaller lots, and their original names appear only on old maps. The hills of southern California still have patches of chaparral

Schoolchildren gather before beginning their tour of Mission San Juan Capistrano.

Two Sides to the Story

Each year the Catholic Church honors a few people whose lives were spent in honest and unselfish devotion to others. The tribute, called beatification, is a step toward becoming a saint. In 1988 the Church extended this honor to Father Junípero Serra.

The tribute offended many Native Americans. They said they didn't want to reward a man who had started a system that destroyed Indian lifeways. To defend the plan, the Church pointed out that Father Serra had devoted his life to the Catholic faith and to sharing his beliefs with others.

The beatification ceremony to honor Father Serra took place in Rome, Italy. Hundreds of people celebrated at San Diego de Alcalá. But 30 Native Americans showed up to express their anger. The Church still stands behind its decision.

Sunlight streams into the church at San Luis Rey de Francia, the only mission church whose dome is still standing.

plants. But the days when California was mostly untouched land are long gone.

Many descendants of mission Indians still hold fast to their ancient culture and heritage. Some are bitterly angry that the California missions caused the death of more than three-fourths of their ancestors. To these descendants, the missions represent the destruction of Indian lifeways and culture. At the same time, many of these Indians are practicing Roman Catholics who have voiced concerns that the Church should make an effort to help people better understand the history of mission Indians.

Some Indians in southern California still live on reservations, while others reside in cities or small towns. Their leaders work hard to give their people a voice in politics and to build businesses that improve the lives of Indians. On the reservations, Native Americans have started casinos and use the money that these businesses earn to build health clinics and schools. Other Indian groups rent their land to farmers and miners.

Throughout California there are reminders of the Franciscan missionaries. For example, the olive groves, vineyards, and wineries that flourish in the state got their start from the Spanish priests. Even the architecture of many local buildings was in part inspired by the California missions.

Some of the most dramatic events in California's history took place beneath the red-tiled roofs and behind the whitewashed adobe walls of the southern coast missions. San Diego de Alcalá, San Juan Capistrano, and San Luis Rey de Francia are places where the past and present come together.

AFTERWORD

Each year thousands of tourists and students visit the California missions. Many of these visitors look around and conclude that the missions are the same today as they were long ago. But, over time, the missions have gone through many changes. The earliest structures were replaced by sturdier buildings with tall towers and long arcades. But even these solid buildings eventually fell into ruin and later were reconstructed.

Our understanding of the missions also has changed through the years. Missionaries, visitors, novelists, and scholars have expressed different opinions about the California missions. These observers often have disagreed about the impact of the missions on the Indians in California. And the voices of Native Americans—from the past *and* the present—have continued to shed light on the mission experience.

The early Franciscan missionaries believed that they were improving the local Indians by introducing them to mission life. But visitors from Europe and the United States frequently described the Spanish missions as cruel places. A French explorer in 1786, for example, reported that the priests treated the neophytes like slaves. He was horrified that Spanish soldiers tracked down runaway Indians and whipped them for trying to return to their old way of life.

Many early visitors were truly concerned about the mistreatment of Native Americans. But the foreign travelers, jealous of Spain's hold on Alta California, also criticized the missions as a way to prove that Spain wasn't worthy to possess the region. Similarly, a young man from the eastern United States, visiting Alta California in the 1830s, was saddened to see so much sickness and death at the missions. He advised his fellow Americans that the region would fare much better as a part of the United States.

The missions were all but forgotten during the 25 years following the U.S. takeover of California. The once solid structures decayed into piles of rotting adobe. One U.S. visitor wrote that she doubted if any structure on earth was "colder, barer, uglier, [or] dirtier" than a California mission.

Just when the missions had disappeared almost completely, they came roaring back to public attention. Beginning in the 1880s, dozens of novels and plays about early California described the Franciscan priests as kind-hearted souls who treated neophytes with gentleness and care. This favorable image of the missions became popular because it gave many Californians a positive sense of their own history and identity. The writings also attracted droves of tourists to California. Merchants and business leaders in the state supported the rebuilding of the crumbling missions because it made good business sense.

The missions today are still the subject of a lively debate. Some people continue to believe that the missions brought many benefits to the Indians by "uplifting" them to European ways. But many others, including some descendants of the neophytes, say that the missions destroyed Native American lifeways and killed thousands of Indians. For all of us, the missions continue to stand as reminders of a difficult and painful time in California history.

Dr. James J. Rawls
Diablo Valley College

CHRONOLOGY

Important Dates in the History of the Missions of the Southern Coast

1542	Juan Rodríguez Cabrillo sails into what is now San Diego Bay and claims it for Spain
1602	Sebastián Vizcaíno names the San Diego Bay
1769	San Diego de Alcalá, the first Franciscan mission in Alta California, is founded
1775	Indians rebel at Mission San Diego; San Juan Capistrano is founded and abandoned
1776	San Juan Capistrano is reestablished
1784	Father Junípero Serra dies; Father Fermín Francisco de Lasuén becomes the new father-president
1798	San Luis Rey de Francia is founded
1810	Revolution begins in New Spain
1812	Earthquake hits the southern coast region
1821	New Spain gains independence from Spain
1830s	Missions are secularized
1846	Mexican War begins; U.S. Navy occupies Monterey
1848	Mexican War ends; Mexico cedes Alta California to the United States
1850	California becomes the thirty-first state
1850s	U.S. government begins to return the California missions to the Catholic Church; mission buildings are falling apart
1890s–present	Missions are restored

ACKNOWLEDGMENTS

Photos, maps, and artworks are used courtesy of: Laura Westlund, pp. 1, 13, 19, 30, 35, 38, 42, 46; © Don Eastman, p. 2; Southwest Museum, Los Angeles, CA, pp. 8–9 (photo by Don Meyer, CT.374–646.G136), p. 27 (22.G.978QCT616); North Wind Picture Archives, p. 10; Independent Picture Service, pp. 12, 31, 32, 34, 36 (right), 47 (inset), 49, 55, 56, 58 (left), 61 (left), 63 (top and bottom), 67 (all), 68 (right); Mount Palomar Winery, p. 15; © Frank Balthis, pp. 16, 17 (inset), 25 (left); © Eda Rogers, pp. 16 (inset), 18, 20 (top and bottom), 22 (left); De Saisset Museum, Santa Clara University/ photo by Diana Peterson, p. 21; © Diana Peterson, p. 22 (right); San Diego Museum of Man, pp. 20 (middle), 23; UPI/Bettmann, p. 25 (right); © Carol Stiver, pp. 26, 37 (bottom), 40, 44 (bottom), 48 (top and bottom), 71 (left); © John Elk III, pp. 28, 39, 47, 50, 73; © Chuck Place, pp. 36 (left), 37 (top), 72 (right); © D. J. Lambrecht, pp. 41, 43 (left), 44 (top), 45; © Shirley Jordan, p. 48 (middle); Mansell Collection, p. 51; California Historical Society, pp. 52, 58 (bottom); Seaver Center for Western History Research, Natural History Museum of Los Angeles County, pp. 57, 66; The Huntington Library, pp. 58 (right), 66 (right); Library of Congress, pp. 61 (right), 66 (left); National Anthropological Archives, Smithsonian Institution, p. 62; San Diego Historical Society Photograph Collection, pp. 63 (middle), 68 (left); California Department of Transportation, McCurry Glassplate #3881, p. 69; San Diego Union Tribune, p. 71 (right); © Lynda Richards, p. 72 (left); Independent Picture Service/Nancy Smedstad, pp. 74–75; Nancy Lemke, p. 78 (top); Dr. James J. Rawls, p. 78 (middle); Professor Edward D. Castillo, p. 78 (bottom). Cover: (Front) © Chuck Place; (Back) Laura Westlund.

Quotations are from the original, translated writings of Father Junípero Serra, pp. 25, 30; Governor Pedro Fages, p. 33; Father Francisco Suñer and Father José Barona, p. 45; Father Fermín Francisco de Lasuén, p. 54; and Governor Juan Bautista Alvarado, p. 60 (both). The quotation on p. 70 is reprinted by permission of Copley News Service.

METRIC CONVERSION CHART

WHEN YOU KNOW	MULTIPLY BY	TO FIND
inches	2.54	centimeters
feet	0.3048	meters
miles	1.609	kilometers
square feet	0.0929	square meters
acres	0.4047	hectares
ounces	28.3495	grams
pounds	0.454	kilograms
gallons	3.7854	liters

ABOUT THE AUTHOR

Nancy Lemke is a writer and artist with a special interest in California history. She has written for children's magazines, and her first book, *Cabrillo, First European Explorer of the California Coast,* was published in 1991. Lemke also owns a book distribution company that promotes children's books about California. She lives in Bonita, California, with her husband and her cat.

ABOUT THE CONSULTANTS

James J. Rawls is one of the most widely published and respected historians in the field of California history. Since 1975 he has been teaching California history at Diablo Valley College. Among his publications are *Indians of California: the Changing Image, New Directions in California History,* and, with Walton Bean, *California: An Interpretive History.* Dr. Rawls is also the author of several works for young readers, including *Never Turn Back: Father Serra's Mission* and *California Dreaming.* Dr. Rawls frequently serves as a consultant for books, for television and radio programs, and for film documentaries on subjects dealing with California's history.

Edward D. Castillo is a direct descendant of Cahuilla-Luiseño Indians who lived at Missions San Gabriel and San Luis Rey. A professor of California Indian ethnohistory for more than 20 years, Castillo offers Native perspectives of mission life to students of California history. His first book is entitled *Native American Perspectives on the Hispanic Colonization of Alta California.* He recently cowrote, with historian Robert Jackson, *Indians, Franciscans and Spanish Colonization: The Impact of the Mission System on California Indians.* Professor Castillo is a founding member of the Native American Studies Departments at the Los Angeles and Berkeley campuses of the University of California. At Sonoma State University, he serves as an associate professor and chairs its Native American Studies Department.

INDEX